T0393362

COUNTEE CULLEN

Poet of the Harlem Renaissance

BLACK ARTISTS

COUNTEE
CULLEN

Poet of the
Harlem Renaissance

Enslow Publishing
101 W. 23rd Street
Suite 240
New York, NY 10011
USA

enslow.com

**CHARLOTTE ETINDE-CROMPTON AND
SAMUEL WILLARD CROMPTON**

Published in 2020 by Enslow Publishing, LLC.
101 W. 23rd Street, Suite 240, New York, NY 10011

Library of Congress Cataloging-in-Publication Data

Names: Crompton, Samuel Willard, author. | Etinde-Crompton, Charlotte, Juvenile literature.
Title: Countee Cullen : poet of the Harlem Renaissance/Samuel Willard Crompton and Charlotte Etinde-Crompton.
Description: New York : Enslow Publishing, 2020. | Series: Celebrating Black artists | Includes bibliographical references and index. | Audience: Grades 7–12.
Identifiers: LCCN 2018016395| ISBN 9781978503557 (library bound) | ISBN 9781978505308 (pbk.)
Subjects: LCSH: Cullen, Countee, 1903–1946—Juvenile literature. | Poets, American—20th century—Biography—Juvenile literature. | African American poets—Biography—Juvenile literature. | Harlem Renaissance—Juvenile literature.
Classification: LCC PS3505.U287 Z58 2018 | DDC 811/.52—dc23
LC record available at https://lccn.loc.gov/2018016395

Printed in China

To Our Readers: We have done our best to make sure all website addresses in this book were active and appropriate when we went to press. However, the author and the publisher have no control over and assume no liability for the material available on those websites or on any websites they may link to. Any comments or suggestions can be sent by e-mail to customerservice@enslow.com.

Photo Credits: Cover, pp. 3, 12–13, 58, 66–67 Bettmann/Getty Images; p. 8 Library of Congress Prints and Photographs Division Washington, D.C.; pp. 11, 27, 79 from the Countee Cullen Papers, courtesy of Amistad Research Center; pp. 16–17 Beyond My Ken/Wikimedia Commons/File:Salem_United_Methodist_Church_211_West_129th_Street.jpg/CC BY-SA 4.0; p. 19 Win McNamee/Getty Images; pp. 23, 30 Private Collection/Prismatic Pictures/Bridgeman Images; p. 32 Underwood Archives/Archive Photos/Getty Images; pp. 34–35 The New York Historical Society/Archive Photos/Getty Images; pp. 38–39 FPG/Archive Photos/Getty Images; pp. 42–43 PhotoQuest/Archive Photos/Getty Images; p. 47 Culture Club/Hulton Archive; pp. 50–51 Science History Images/Alamy Stock Photo; pp. 54–55 Fay 2018/Alamy Stock Photo; pp. 62–63 Hulton Archive/Getty Images; pp. 70–71 Keystone-France/Gamma-Keystone/Getty Images; p. 74–75 ullstein bild Dtl./Getty Images; pp. 76–77 Science History Images/Alamy Stock Photo; pp. 82–83 Historic Map Works LLC/Getty Images; pp. 86–87 Al Fenn/The LIFE Picture Collection/Getty Images; p. 89 New York Daily News Archive/Getty Images.

Contents

Pained Youth

Any biography of Countee Cullen must begin with a disclaimer: there is much we do not know. Though it would be convenient to blame the march of time, or the loss of precious documents, a majority of the responsibility has to be assigned to the poet himself: Cullen kept many things private, and some he took to the grave.

Did it have to be this way? Poets are sensitive, almost by definition, and the pain of Cullen's early life led him to conceal things we wish could see the light of day. But poets, as well as writers of prose, often leave a body of work that allows others to see into their life, and so it is with Countee Cullen. One of the most revealing of his early poems, published in 1925, is "Saturday's Child": "Some are teethed on a silver spoon/ With the stars strung for a rattle;/ I cut my teeth as the black raccoon—/ For implements of battle."[1] It's not difficult to see that Cullen knew struggle and hard work.

Birth and Earliest Years

Throughout life, Cullen claimed to have been born in New York City. Not only is there no supporting evidence, but the

Though he claimed to have been a lifelong New Yorker, Countee Cullen was actually born in Louisville, Kentucky.

fragments that remain suggest he was born in Louisville, Kentucky. The year is typically believed to have been 1903, and the date appears to have been May 30. What *is* known—beyond the shadow of a doubt—is that Countee Cullen was not the biological son of Reverend Frederick A. Cullen and Carolyn Belle Mitchell. They adopted him about the age of fifteen, and acted very much as if they were his parents, but there was no blood connection. Countee Cullen was very sensitive about this point, to where many people—even his good friends—did not realize that he had not always lived in a sober, serious, and respectable middle-class household.

In fact, the truth was quite different. In-depth research, executed over many years, indicates that Countee Cullen was born Countee Porter, and that the earliest spelling of his name may have been the phonetic "County." Almost certainly, Countee was born in Louisville, Kentucky, but he did not remain there very long. His father appears to have abandoned the family when Countee was quite young. Countee went to live with his grandmother in New York City.

Amanda Porter was a daycare worker in Manhattan. On the few occasions when he spoke of her, Cullen remembered his grandmother with great fondness. Like many African American women of the time, she struggled to make ends meet, but she seems to have given him the closest he had to real family feeling, prior to his adoption by the Cullens. In his first book of poetry, Cullen honored her memory with these lines:

> This lovely flower fell to seed;
> Work gently, sun and rain;

> She held it as her dying creed
> That she would grow again.[2]

The chances are that Cullen was raised in a pious atmosphere, that his grandmother instructed him in the Bible. Though he later showed skepticism where the Bible and Christian beliefs are concerned, there is little doubt Cullen was deeply influenced by her.

A Sensitive Child

Though photographs of family members are lacking, there is precisely one photo of young Countee Cullen, and it reveals more than one can find from the literary and documentary sources: Young Countee Cullen, then Countee Porter, stands in the doorway of an apartment building. He holds a book in his hands, and may be on the verge of reciting a line or two of poetry.

His extraordinary sensitivity is obvious. The boy, who looks to be the age of nine, stands in the shy introverted posture of many children, while his face reveals a deep and sad soul. Here is a person who already knows his personhood, who feels quite different from the other children of the neighborhood.

Countee wears a white shirt and tie. This may be an important day at school; equally, it could be an important event at church. In either case, this photograph provides us with real insight into the young Countee Cullen—he already shows the posture of his later years. This helps explain his phenomenal success at school.

New York City school records are far from complete, but they do show that Countee moved from one school to another, as his grandmother moved from one address to

Countee's adoptive mother, Carolyn Mitchell Cullen, is shown to the right.

another. The one truly consistent thing about Cullen's elementary school years is the incredible promise he showed. Regardless of where he attended, Cullen was at or near the top of his class.

The Silent Parade

Very likely, Countee Cullen was mostly concerned with his grandmother, his home, and his days at school. But he cannot have completely escaped the outside world. Almost certainly, he knew about the transition from peace to war—the beginning of the First World War—and of the struggles experienced by many African Americans.

America entered the Great War—as it was then called—in April 1917. Tens of thousands of African Americans quickly enlisted in the Army and Navy, only to experience segregation and racism. Many shrugged, saying there was nothing they could do, but a handful of African American leaders in New York City declared something had to be done. They organized the Silent Parade.

On a July day in 1917, ten thousand African Americans—men, women, and children—made a silent march up through midtown Manhattan. Through their march, and the silence they

On July 28, 1917, around ten thousand African American citizens participated in the Silent March to protest segregation and racism in the US military.

Is Genius Born or Made?

When one takes Countee Cullen as the example, one leans to the former of the two. Very likely, Cullen did not have access to many books in his youth. Almost certainly he did not have a friendly or helpful hand from an older, wiser relative. Instead, his natural gift for language, and for poetry in particular, seems to have sprung right out of his own DNA. Of course one can find examples to the contrary: young people who make themselves into scholars. But Cullen appears to have been born for the role he played.

observed, these black citizens protested the shame of segregation, and the violence that had recently taken place in the city of East St. Louis.

Was Countee Cullen among the teenagers that marched? It is entirely possible. Whether Countee participated or not, he was about to be swept up by certain events. These would land him in a most fortunate position, as the adopted son of one of Harlem's most important religious leaders.

A New Life

Anyone who studies Countee Cullen's life comes to marvel at his extreme good fortune. This didn't come without sadness and great loss: In 1917, Amanda Porter, Cullen's grandmother, passed away. His grandmother's death could have been the prelude to a miserable time; it could even have doomed him to poverty and obscurity. Instead, at the age of fifteen, he was suddenly adopted by the most prominent minister in Harlem.

Self-Made Man

Frederick Asbury Cullen's story is one of the great rags-to-riches tales. Born in rural Maryland in 1868, he was the youngest of eleven children, and both of his parents had previously been slaves. Frederick Cullen later described his early life:

> My father died when I was two months old....Not being able to care properly for all of the children, I was therefore the one most neglected. I wore dresses until quite a large boy, and I did not even

Frederick Cullen was the pastor at the Salem Methodist Episcopal Church in Harlem for forty years.

have shoes to wear until I was six or seven years old. The first time I ever attended Sunday school or church was while my mother went to visit. I ran away and went to Sunday School barefoot. I stopped and washed my bare feet in the ditch and wiped them with grass and weeds and went on to the church.[1]

Though this was obviously an intense experience, hardship tales like his were all-too-common in late nineteenth-century America. The really remarkable thing is that he was able to escape those circumstances, and elevate himself.

Through sheer force of will, Frederick Cullen made it through junior college and became a teacher in Maryland. Continued, repeated concerns over his vocation led him to return to college. When he was ordained a Methodist pastor in 1900, his career seemed assured. Even so, Cullen's first days in New York City were less than auspicious, as he described in his autobiography:

On April 18, 1902, I landed in New York...I was to take

> charge of the mission in Harlem. It had been started and was under the supervision of St. Mark's. The next day, which was Saturday, I went in search of the mission that I was to take charge of. Dr. Brooks sent with me a young man whose name I do not recall. We reached St. Nicholas Avenue, as we were informed that the mission church was in that neighborhood. We looked, looked, and looked for the church, passing it by several times looking for it. Finally we saw a slate in the window of a little store. Believing this to be the church, we went up to it and found out it was.[2]

Few young pastors would welcome such a beginning, but Reverend Cullen was a person of tremendous willpower. In a matter of months, he increased the congregation from three to a few dozen, and in a matter of years, he became one of the most visible persons on the streets of Harlem. Taking his ministry to the streets, Reverend Cullen played marbles with young boys, told them stories of Christ's glory, and managed to get them to go to his church.

Reverend Cullen was almost entirely self-made. What he lacked in sophistication was made up for by his indefatigable spirit and willingness. By the time he took Countee Cullen as his adopted son, Frederick Cullen was one of the most respected men in Harlem.

Finding a Family

Carolyn Belle Mitchell was a singer and pianist from Baltimore. Sadly, our knowledge of their courtship is limited to what Reverend Cullen declared in his autobiography:

> I went to Atlantic City for a little vacation, went to Asbury M.E. Church to a concert. Lo and

Leading the Way

Reverend Cullen came to know many, if not most, of the major leaders of Harlem's African American community. In 1917, he helped organize the Silent Parade, and in 1918 he traveled to Washington, DC, to help persuade President Woodrow Wilson to commute the sentences of African American soldiers accused of rioting in a white town. In addition, Reverend Cullen was both an early organizer of the National Association for the Advancement of Colored People (NAACP), and the president of its New York City chapter. Reverend Cullen's achievements were not quite the equal of those of scholar W. E. B. Du Bois, but as a moral voice, his was second to none.

> behold, there was this woman with the challis dress and pompadour brown hair, singing, singing, yes, singing [Reverend Cullen had previously had a dream of a woman like this one]....So I met her, Miss Carolyn Belle Mitchell of Baltimore. Believing and knowing that I had met the correct woman, that the Lord had selected her for me. It was love at first sight, at least on my part.[3]

From that swift beginning developed a marriage that lasted nearly three decades. Carolyn Cullen was of inestimable assistance to her husband in all ways. There was only one great sadness for them both. They had no children and had just about given up the effort when Reverend Cullen learned of a youngster in his parish who had just been orphaned. This was Countee Cullen.

Adoption

The precise facts surrounding the adoption are hazy at best. All one can say for certain is that Countee Cullen's grandmother—Amanda Porter—died toward the end of November 1917 and that Countee was adopted into the Cullen household sometime in early 1918.

What developed was a relationship of great affection between child and parents. Though he was the youngest of the trio, Countee was in many ways the star. He was the child the parents had always looked for, and his native intelligence and gift at self-expression, was already developed by the time he entered the Cullen home. There were conflicts, between the expressive, sometimes high-living son and the sober, respectable parents, but Countee Cullen was always careful to show respect for his adopted parents. He wrote several poems in his father's honor, the

Religious Conflict

Years after his adoption, Countee Cullen asserted that the major conflict of his life lay in reconciling a calm and conservative religious upbringing with a pagan inclination. Countee was a Christian, but a most unorthodox one, while his father was a true religious conservative. Remarkably, the divergence between their religious inclinations did not damage their relationship. If anything, father and adopted son grew closer with the passing of the years.

longest of which, entitled "Dad," touches on his father's religiosity and guidance: "His words are sage and fall with care/ Because he loves me so,/ And being his, he knows, I fear,/ The dizzy path I go."[4]

The dizzy path refers to the bewildering variety of social options Countee Cullen enjoyed in his twenties. His way was not circumspect and bound, like his adoptive father's. But even the young Countee Cullen recognized the worth of what his father had done in life.

> Then when the star has shed its gleam,
>   The rose its crimson coat,
> When Beauty flees the hidden dream
>   And Pans pipes blow no note,
> When both my shoes are worn too thin
>   My weight of fire to bear,
> I'll turn like dad and like him win
>   The peace of a snug arm-chair.[5]

3

Prodigy

Aspects of Countee Cullen's life can be compared to those of the prodigal son in the Bible. Like that young man, Cullen lived fast and hard, sometimes regretting his decisions. But one can also call Cullen the *prodigious* and *prolific* son, because of his hard work and significant achievements at an early age.

First Poem

Cullen had been writing poems for some time before he first saw publication. This came in a high school magazine in 1918, just as he was transferring from Townsend Harris High School to DeWitt Clinton High. A teacher at Townsend accepted a challenge from a friend who declared young students incapable of writing poems. Countee Cullen proved he was more than capable. "To the Swimmer" shows a young mind in the making:

> Now as I watch you, strong of arm and endurance,
>   battling and struggling
> With the waves that rush against you, ever with
>   invincible strength returning

Countee Cullen showed promise as a poet even as a young high school student.

Into my heart, grown each day, more tranquil and
    peaceful, comes a fierce longing
Of mind and soul that will not be appeased until,
    like you,
I breast yon deep and boundless expanse of blue.
With an outward stroke of power intense your mighty
    arm goes forth,
Cleaving its way through waters that rise and roll,
    ever a ceaseless vigil keeping
Over the treasures beneath.
My heart goes out to you of dauntless courage
    and spirit indomitable,
And though my lips would speak, my spirit forbids
    me to ask,
"Is your heart as true as your arm?"[1]

For a boy of fifteen, this poem was truly an impressive accomplishment. Cullen's new teachers at Dewitt Clinton High School became ever more aware of his talent.

Overcoming Bias

Cullen had been an underdog throughout life: this is expressed both in his poems and his letters. But at DeWitt Clinton High School, he was also a noticeable minority, one of only a few dozen young black men in a school of nearly six thousand.

To a great degree, Cullen managed to find his way round the bias that existed. He was very active in extracurricular activities, working on the school newspaper, and writing poems, both for publication and private consumption. The one photograph that survives shows Cullen with about forty of his classmates, all of them white. There is a decided sadness in his face, but there is also a sense of success. The young poet was finding his way. Never was this better expressed than in "I Have a Rendezvous with Life."

In 1919, Cullen penned this poem, partly in response to "I Have a Rendezvous with Death." The latter poem had been written three years earlier, by a young American volunteer serving with the French army in World War I. Alan Seeger, uncle of the famed singer and songwriter Pete Seeger, wrote his poem while serving on the front lines, and his words soon proved prophetic: he died on the Western Front. Cullen penned his own poem in response.

> I have a rendezvous with life,
> In days I hope will come,
> Ere youth has sped and strength of mind;
> Ere voices sweet grow dumb;
> I have a rendezvous with life,
> When spring's first heralds hum.
>
> It may be I shall greet her soon,
> Shall riot at her bedside;
> It may be I shall seek in vain
> The peace of her downy breast;
> Yet I would keep this rendezvous,
> And count all hardships sweet,
> If at the end of the long white way,
> There life and I shall meet.
>
> Sure some will cry it better far
> To crown their days with sleep,
> Than face the wind the road and rain,
> To heed the calling deep:
> Though wet nor blow nor space I fear,
> Yet fear I deeply too,

> Lest Death shall greet and claim me ere
> I keep Life's rendezvous.[2]

Though he was still a young poet learning the finer points of his craft, the sentiment is powerful and plain. Here is a young man who knows that death comes all too soon, and that he needs to keep alive—mentally and spiritually as well as physically—in order to accomplish his goal before the end. "I Have a Rendezvous with Life" was printed in several New York City newspapers, and Countee Cullen's name began to reach beyond the confines of the Salem Methodist Church and DeWitt Clinton High School.

Finding His Place

Countee Cullen had a decided gift for friendship. Even in junior high school, he formed strong bonds with other boys, and the friends exchanged letters for the rest of their lives. At DeWitt Clinton High, Cullen met the man who would be his most constant and devoted friend, Harold Jackman.

Born in London to a Jamaican mother and a half-German father, Jackman arrived in New York City in time for high school (he was one year ahead of Countee Cullen at DeWitt Clinton High). Handsome, debonair, and self-assured, Jackman was everything Countee Cullen was not, and the same can be said in the other direction (Jackman never excelled in his studies, for example). Despite their differences, the two young men became fast friends, and their letters indicate a high level of emotional intimacy. Of course, this raises another question: was there physical intimacy as well?

Cullen and Harold Jackman were deep and close friends for twenty-five years; while it's unclear if they were

After meeting at DeWitt Clinton High School, Harold Jackman and Countee Cullen would become close friends for the remainder of their lives.

physically intimate, there is much to suggest a strong, possibly romantic relationship. However, there is also evidence that Countee Cullen did have intimate relationships with other men. Cullen was tortured, conflicted about his sexuality. While he would go on to marry two women, it's widely believed that he privately identified as a gay man, one who felt it necessary, for obvious reasons, to stay deeply closeted, only fully revealing himself through his letters to friends such as Alain Locke.

Graduating from DeWitt Clinton High School in 1921, Countee Cullen found himself in strong demand. His poetic record spoke for itself, and his grades in most other subjects were good to excellent. Cullen won a New York State Regents scholarship, which he hoped to use to attend Columbia University. Columbia did not accept his application, however, and Cullen went to New York University. Every indication was that Cullen would equal, and perhaps exceed, his high school accomplishments.

Recognition

How far had Countee Cullen come by the age of twenty? Despite a rough, even painful, start in life, he had come about as far as any young African American intellectual of his time. The only people he could look to as mentors were significantly older.

Alain Locke

The date they first met is unknown. What can be said, with confidence, is that Alain Locke represented the type of success, and acclaim, that Countee Cullen dreamed of. Born into middle-class circumstances in Philadelphia, Locke was the most exquisitely educated African American of his generation. He graduated from Harvard, earned a degree from Oxford, and was America's first black Rhodes Scholar (the next one did not emerge till the 1950s). Handsome, charming, and shrewd, Locke had everything going for him except personal happiness. He was a gay

Scholar and writer Alain Locke often helped to nurture young black artists, forming a deep friendship with Cullen.

The Unique Struggle of Gay Black Men

With the hindsight of almost one hundred years, it is relatively easy to see that some leading African American poets, singers, and intellectuals were homosexual. But during the 1920s and 1930s, it was almost impossible to see this. Because of the systematic, continued oppression that was a part of daily life for black men and women, African American society expected even greater demonstrations of strength and masculinity from black men (even while that very masculinity was considered threatening by white society). In the context of his home, a man was supposed to be the king, in charge of all that he surveyed. Being gay in the 1920s presented challenges for all men, but for black men in particular. Homosexuality—which could (or could not) include a softer, more feminine presentation in speech and affect—was especially difficult to reconcile with the strength needed to lead a black family living under the cloud of codified racism and discrimination. For many decades beyond the 1920s and 1930s, gay black men have faced the pressures of remaining closeted to preserve a false image of masculinity, an image that didn't allow for a strong black man to also be gay.

Like his good friend Langston Hughes (*pictured above*), Countee Cullen worked in the food service industry as a young man.

man, in a time when it was almost impossible to come out of the closet.

Alain Locke first came to New York City to visit Cullen. He found him at NYU, and visited the Cullen home, where Reverend Cullen was furious at having missed his opportunity to meet the academic legend. Cullen spent the spring break of his junior year in Washington, DC, where he lived with Locke.

Were they lovers? Very likely so. But both men treasured a discreet quality, an ability to keep their private lives private. There is, therefore, no letter that lays out the exact details of their relationship. Locke was fairly crazy about Countee Cullen, but there was a second object to his desire. He was also very attracted to Langston Hughes, an up-and-coming black poet who studied briefly at Columbia University. Countee Cullen was the go-between, the person who knew both Locke and Langston Hughes. Whether he really wanted Locke to meet Hughes can be questioned. What can be said is that Cullen and Hughes went separate ways in the summer of 1924, leaving Alain Locke rather lonely and frustrated. This is known from a letter Locke wrote to Cullen: "Naturally I am depressed. You as a bus-boy and Langston as galley-slave—when I had in imagination placed the trio in Europe this summer."[1] The reference to working as a waiter was not figurative—Cullen was working as a waiter in Atlantic City. Cullen used this summer job to illuminate his poetry: With subtle poise he grips his tray/ Of delicate things to eat;/ Choice viands to their mouths half way,/ The ladies watch his feet.[2] The poem is not a masterpiece, but it does its work admirably. Cullen goes to the root of the matter (his African heritage

Cullen earned his undergraduate degree from New York University in 1925.

and descent) but he also shows his dislike for middle-class society.

The summer at Atlantic City makes more sense when one realizes that Cullen's adoptive father had performed the same job, twenty-five years earlier. Quite possibly, Reverend Cullen insisted on this summer of waiting tables as a character-building exercise.

Travel Plans

As graduation from NYU approached, Cullen did his best to finance a year abroad. His strongest desire was to become a Rhodes Scholar, but though he shaped and reshaped his application, it ultimately failed to win acceptance. At the same time, Cullen considered an advanced degree. Reverend Frederick Cullen yearned for his adopted son to become a PhD, to hold a doctorate. This was not Countee Cullen's goal, at least not right away. Cullen agreed to apply to Harvard University for a master's program, but that was as much as he would allow.

Color

Countee Cullen's time at Harvard University was relatively short. He earned his master's degree in one year. To be sure, Cullen was thrilled to be part of an academic tradition stretching back almost three hundred years. But Harvard was less important to his development than either DeWitt Clinton High School or New York University. By the time he arrived in Boston, Cullen had developed his talent and his approach to his work. Then, too, he had become one of the foremost of all African American poets, with the publication of *Color*.

A Stunning Debut

In October 1925, Cullen's first book of poems, *Color*, was published by Harper & Brothers of New York. Cullen was by no means the first African American poet to break into print, but he did so in an astounding manner. Seldom, if ever, was so much critical attention—much of it positive— lavished on a first book.

Coming in at 108 pages, *Color* did not overwhelm with size or length. Rather, it invited the reader into Countee

Though he studied at Harvard University, Cullen was already a published poet when he entered its hallowed halls.

Harvard Union - Harvard College

Cullen's inner life, and did so in a way that promised even greater things for the future. After dedicating the book to his parents, Cullen went straight to the heart of the matter. "Incident" describes one of his earliest, and most painful, experiences:

> Once riding in old Baltimore,
>> Heart-filled, head-filled with glee,
> I saw a Baltimorean
>> Keep looking straight at me.
> Now I was eight and very small,
>> And he was no whit bigger,
> And so I smiled, but he poked out
>> His tongue, and called me, "Nigger."
> I saw the whole of Baltimore
>> From May until December;
> Of all I things that happened there
>> That's all that I remember.[1]

This was a stirring account of the psychological wounds inflicted by institutional racism. Turn of the twentieth century African Americans were used to being ignored—it went with the territory. But along with the averted gaze sometimes came the penetrating and angry stare, followed by the racial expletive. Was it truly just one event Cullen remembered, or did he compile several, and use poetic license? In either case, he captured the moment, and preserved it for his reader.

Color featured much new poetry, but it also reprinted a handful of earlier poems. Cullen had already paid tribute to his adoptive father, but he went further, addressing both parents in "Fruit of the Flower," gently dissecting the currents of desire and longing underneath their piety. He then wonders how, filled with their own yearning, they can question the subjects and leanings of his poetry:

> Why should she think it devil's art
>> That all my songs should be
> Of love and lovers, broken heart,
>> And wild sweet agony?
> Who plants a seed begets a bud,
>> Extract of that same root;
> Why marvel at the hectic blood
>> That flushes this wild fruit?[2]

This is about as self-descriptive as Countee Cullen gets. He sensed, perhaps knew, that it was not his fate to live a calm or sedate life like his adoptive father. His poetic gift needed the constant refreshment of society, and of Harlem society at its most extravagant.

Cullen's "The Shroud of Color" is one of the most painful poems describing black identity in America, penetrating to the core of an ingrained sense of inadequacy driven by institutional racism: "Lord, being dark, forewilled to that despair/ My color shrouds me in, I am as dirt/ Beneath my brother's heel."[3]

Here, Cullen brings together all the strands of his biography—poverty, pained youth, Christianity, and despair—and welds them into one great piece of work. The poem goes on, using symbolic imagery such as "the many-colored coat of dreams," and Cullen continues to address God, saying being black in white America is simply too painful. For Cullen, God answers: " 'Dark child of sorrow, mine no less, what art/ Of mine can make thee see and play thy part?/ They key to all strange things is in thy heart.'"[4]

The Harlem Renaissance saw a bloom of artistry and creativity in all disciplines: writing, visual art, and music.

The Harlem Renaissance

Most observers of the Harlem Renaissance agree that it began in the 1920s, and that 1925 represented its flood tide. *Color* was published to great acclaim, as was Alain Locke's *The New Negro*. The social life of Harlem hit a peak a year or two later, with more nightclubs and poetry readings than ever before. Countee Cullen certainly gave his best efforts to the Harlem Renaissance, and helped that movement gain strength, but he also benefited from its activity. If there had not been so many eager readers in Harlem and such a robust artistic culture blooming, Cullen would be much less known today.

Here, Cullen brings the voice of God in a style like that of the Book of Job, in the Old Testament.

Like Job, the narrator of the poem, perhaps Countee Cullen himself, decides to live, to taste all the experience his heavenly father can give.

The Critical Response

Most critics were positive: *Color* was an outstanding debut, they declared, and if Cullen continued on this track, he would surely become one of the great twentieth-century poets. The few that disagreed tended to criticize the poetic style rather than the message. Cullen's poetry was too stilted, they declared, too reminiscent of the poetry learned in the classroom. What they did not realize was that Cullen had already become the poet he would be. He could no more change his style, at the age of twenty-three, than a skilled athlete can alter his physique.

From one quarter came a thunder of applause. Those who knew Alain Locke thought him incapable of exaggeration: his responses were nearly always measured and balanced. But this was not the case with *Color*: Locke enthused about the book in a review written for the African American journal, *Opportunity*:

> Ladies and gentlemen! A genius! Posterity will laugh at us if we do not proclaim him now. COLOR transcends all of the limiting qualifications that might be brought forward if it were merely a work of talent...It is the work of a Negro poet writing for the most part out of the intimate emotional experience of race, but the adjective is for the first time made irrelevant, so thoroughly has he poeticized the substance and fused it with the universally human moods of life.[5]

If another person made such a statement, one would be inclined to dismiss it by half. But Locke had already shown himself *the* man of talent of one generation, and he seemed ready to hand the baton to young Countee Cullen.

The Summit

By January 1926, Countee Cullen had come further than any other young African American writer of his generation. He knew that Alain Locke was the greater scholar, and that Langston Hughes had more direct experience of life on which to draw. But in terms of critical acclaim, Cullen was at the very summit. Given that he was only twenty-three, it seemed likely he had another thirty or forty years to go. Of course, there were whispers of Cullen being unready to take on the mantle of great African American writer. Most of these comments were based on his sexual identity.

Father and Son

Countee Cullen and his adoptive father were about as different as father and son could be. The former was light-hearted, enthusiastic, and sometimes frivolous, while the latter was serious, sober, and sometimes dour. In one respect, they were well-matched, however: both attracted disquieting rumors.

By his twenties, Countee Cullen was already a celebrated and highly regarded poet.

That Reverend Frederick Cullen was a great man was almost impossible to argue. Almost single-handedly, he took the Salem Methodist Church and expanded it—in physical size and congregation—by more than 1,000 percent. But throughout the years of his unquestioned success, Reverend Cullen was also the subject of many rumors, mostly having to do with his sexuality and gender performance.

Not a shred of proof was ever offered. Instead, the gossip merely continued, year after year, causing a tremor in the usual orderly life at the parsonage. People whispered that Reverend Cullen was fond of his wife's clothing and sometimes applied her lipstick to his own face. With the passage of roughly one century, it is virtually impossible to say if the rumors were true. What we can say, with clarity, is that if the rumors were true, the Reverend Cullen would have had to deny them: as a man of the cloth and a prominent black leader, he had no other choice.

That Countee Cullen had a tortured sexuality is almost impossible to dispute. While he had relationships with women and may have even found them attractive, his deepest emotional intimacy was with men. During the years that followed the publication of *Color*, Countee found it impossible to keep speculation at bay. As Harlem's most eligible bachelor, he needed to seek a wife.

Father and Daughter

Countee Cullen first met Yolande Du Bois in 1923. The only daughter of W. E. B. Du Bois, she enjoyed both a privileged and a pained upbringing. Her parents' marriage was not happy, and she grew up feeling a great deal of emotional strain. As the only daughter, and only living child, of the famous black activist, she had to find a man that was her equal.

Cullen and Du Bois liked each other right away. He had a disarming sense of humor, and she was eager to see the best in people. But even during the early months of their courtship, Cullen wrote more revealing letters to his friend Harold Jackman than to his prospective bride. Yolande was a fine person, with a good heart, he wrote. Even with the passage of a century, one can hear, or feel, the limited praise.

Certainly, no one forced Cullen and Yolande to the altar. Both felt the pressure of the African American community, however, and both felt the need to pay something back for all they had received. In Cullen's case, a major overseas trip seems to have been the turning point.

The Cullens Abroad

In 1926, Salem Methodist Church honored its longtime pastor with the gift of an all-paid visit to Europe and the Holy Land. The congregation intended for Reverend Frederick and Mrs. Cullen to take the trip, but the pastor's wife was adamant: she would not take an ocean voyage. Reverend Cullen therefore asked his son, and they decided to leave in July. A revealing diary entry was written by Reverend Cullen on the day of their disembarkation in France:

> Docked at three o'clock in the morning. Countee, my son, with friends of his, namely: Prof. Alain Locke of Howard University, Miss Dorothy Peterson, William Bond, and Arthur Fauset, paid the head steward to permit them to go off board

From left: W. E. B. Du Bois, a young Yolande Du Bois, and Nina Du Bois.

and see the city of Havre. They remained quite late indeed. I remained on board the ship.[1]

Certainly, there was nothing terrible about this one event. But a pattern was set. Countee and his friends celebrated and partied a good deal during the seven-week vacation, while the reverend lived as quietly and abstemiously as if he were back home in his parsonage.

Paris and Marseilles—the latter in the south of France—were the highlights for Countee, while Jerusalem and the Pyramids were the outstanding success for the reverend. The little party saw the Wailing Wall in Jerusalem, but also King Tutankhamen's tomb in Egypt. The reader of Countee's letters suspects that the poet was eager to get back to Paris, and the party returned that way. The difference between father and adopted son is shown by their approach to the use—and carriage—of holy water.

"We had much difficulty in bringing the water home," Reverend Cullen wrote. "The customs officials in Kantara thought it was liquor which was forbidden, but we convinced them that it was water by breaking the seal and permitting them to drink a bit of it. Jacob's Well is about 32 meters deep, which is 100 feet. Water is constantly springing and bubbling up…We also saw the place where Christ was lost from his parents in the crowd."[2]

Reverend Cullen was a literal Christian who believed in the specific application of the Bible. His adopted son was a very loose type of Christian, who understood the Bible in an allegorical sense. Countee's letters to Harold Jackman—whose presence he greatly missed—are filled with fun pokes at Reverend Cullen's literal beliefs.

Jerusalem represented the peak for Reverend Cullen, but Paris was number-one for his adopted son. Paris was "all it ought to be and I am completely ravished by it,"[3] Cullen wrote to Jackman. In this, Countee Cullen and his father were in accord. Both felt an unusual freedom in their blackness while in Paris, a sense that race did not matter. Despite the differences in their approach to religion, father and son became closer during the 1926 tour. It was so satisfactory, in fact, that they made the voyage a dozen times after that.

Sophomore Success

Cullen's second book of poems was published in 1927. *Copper Sun* looked very much like *Color*, with one major difference: the former had pen and ink drawings that served to illustrate the whole. The drawings were created by Charles Cullen (no relation to the author). Issued by Harper & Brothers, *Copper Sun* attracted a favorable, though not adoring, press.

Most critics—of 1927 and our own time—believe that the very first poem, "From the Dark Tower," printed on page three, is the best of the group: "We shall not always plant while others reap/ The golden increment of bursting fruit,/ Not always countenance, abject and mute,/ That lesser men should hold their brothers cheap."[4] The tone is angrier than *Color*. There is nothing specific that happened in 1925 or 1926 accounts for Cullen's changed approach, or at least nothing known to the public. But it is quite possible that Cullen's personal anguish over racial inequality intensified over time.

Countee and Frederick Cullen embarked on a long overseas journey, with Jacob's Well in Jerusalem serving as a memorable stop.

From Three to Two

Countee Cullen and his adoptive stepfather became closer with each trip they made overseas. When Carolyn Belle Mitchell Cullen died in 1932, Reverend Cullen came to need his adopted son even more. The oddity of their different approaches to religion continued, but their mutual affection increased.

The Proposal

Soon after his return to Harlem, Countee Cullen felt more pressure than in the past. He had stunned the literary world with *Color*, and many people believed he needed to surpass, or at least duplicate its effect. Cullen was, indeed, at work on another book of poems, but he also had marriage in mind.

Around Christmas of 1927, Cullen went to the Du Bois home, where he formally asked W. E. B. Du Bois for his daughter's hand in marriage. Du Bois had, indeed, been raised in a time when that formality was necessary, but he regarded himself as a modern, twentieth-century man. "Go ask the girl,"[5] he replied.

Cullen proposed. Yolande accepted. The stage was set for the largest social event of the decade.

Wedding of the Decade

Easter Monday fell on the ninth of April in 1928. The week following the high religious holiday was usually something of a letdown. This was not the case in 1928, however, because Harlem's finest young poet married the daughter of the African American community's most renowned leader.

Father of the Bride

While the father of the groom, Frederick Asbury Cullen, was Harlem's best known man of the cloth, the father of the bride—William Edward Burghardt Du Bois—had an even higher social profile. Born in western Massachusetts in 1869, Du Bois raised himself to become the first black person to earn a PhD from Harvard University. The author of numerous books, Du Bois was best known for his belief that the "Talented Tenth" needed to lead African Americans forward. In every racial or ethnic group there was a concentrated group of talent, Du Bois declared, and it was the ministers, educators, thinkers, and artists who would do so for black citizens.

W. E. B. Du Bois was quite likely the best-known black scholar and writer of the early twentieth century.

After losing a son in infancy, Du Bois and his wife had only one remaining child, Yolande. For more than twenty years, Yolande carried the special burden of representing her father—and his elevated ideals—as well as her young self. That burden of loneliness was about to end because she accepted the proposal of Countee Cullen. Together, these two young people would comfort and help one another, while acting as leaders of the Talented Tenth. At least that was the plan.

Mother of the Groom; Mother of the Bride

Because they were married to very purposeful, forceful, and ambitious men, the mother of the groom and the mother of the bride took secondary, even tertiary, roles in the wedding of their two children. To the best of our knowledge, they were not consulted about the wedding details, which were arranged by W. E. B. Du Bois and his intended son-in-law, Countee Cullen. About the only place where their feminine touch was shown concerned the music to be played. Carolyn Belle Mitchell Cullen was an accomplished singer, whose voice was heard in the Salem Methodist choir. Very likely, it was the mother of the groom who found the organist, and persuaded him to donate his services, as a wedding gift to the young couple.

A Grand Event

After extensive planning, the event was scheduled for 6 p.m. on Easter Monday. One thousand and three hundred official invitations were stamped, and tickets provided, but it soon became apparent there was no way to keep out the curious. All of Harlem knew about the event.

The doors of Salem Methodist opened precisely at 5 p.m., and the ticket holders were ushered in by twelve resplendent young men, friends of the groom. Langston Hughes complained of the necessity to rent a tuxedo, but this was one occasion on which he fulfilled social convention to the letter.

At 5:30, it was discovered that all the ticket holders had been admitted, and the doors were swung wide open to admit roughly one thousand five hundred other people, who had nothing more than curiosity or interest to propel them. By 6 p.m., Salem Methodist was completely filled.

Accompanied by no fewer than sixteen bridesmaids, Yolande Du Bois came to the altar, to be met by Countee Cullen. The actual ceremony was performed by two ministers: Reverend Cullen and Reverend George Frazier Miller. But first came the music.

Melville Charlton was the first African American admitted to the American Society of Organists. Friendly with both of the principal families, he offered his services for free. The organ music began precisely at 6:07 p.m. and commenced with two selections of European classical music. Charlton then moved to "On Bended Knee," an African American favorite. A fifteen-year-old soprano (one of the bride's high school students) sang Cadman's "At Dawning."

The bride wore a cream satin gown trimmed with Duchess lace; white silk hose and satin pumps to match. The lace handkerchief and the lace on her long veil were used by her mother. On her head was a coronet of orange blossoms. Artistically tacked on the two-layer train of satin and net were orange blossoms.[1]

Reverend Frederick Cullen opened the ceremony, and Reverend George Miller pronounced the blessing on the bride and groom. All that remained was the lavish reception, intended for a more intimate five hundred guests.

Praise for the Event

Yolande Du Bois required little introduction, whether in person or in the newspapers. But the African American press made much of her father's accomplishments, and it also praised the young Countee Cullen, as "one of the youngest, and most widely read Negro poets."[2] But the strongest praise came from the father of the bride himself.

W. E. B. Du Bois had taught at Atlanta University before coming north to edit *The Crisis*, an African American periodical which recorded the perils of the time, and the possibilities of a hopeful future. As editor, Du Bois had many occasions to dwell on the frightful conditions faced by many African Americans; lynchings, for example, had grown in number throughout the young century. But as he mused on his only living child, and her fortunate marriage, Du Bois was more than positive.

The symbolism of that procession was tremendous. It was not the mere marriage of a maiden. It was not simply the wedding of a fine young poet. It was

The Harlem of the 1920s was undeniably vibrant, a seemingly perfect home for the new Cullen-Du Bois family.

the symbolic march of young and black America. America, because there was Harvard, Columbia, Smith, Brown, Howard, Chicago, Syracuse, Penn and Cornell. There were three Masters of Arts and fourteen Bachelors. There were poets and teachers, actors, artists and students, But it was not simply conventional America—it had a dark and shimmering beauty all its own; a calm and high restraint and sense of new power; it was a new race; a new thought; a new thing rejoicing in a ceremony as old as the world.[3]

Known for his intense seriousness, Du Bois allowed himself a touch of frivolity, noticing that some of his daughter's bridesmaids smoked cigarettes, a thing unheard of a generation before.

Surprising Results

W. E. B. Du Bois was correct in several respects. The African American community *had* come a long way in his lifetime, and there was certainly hope that its material circumstances would improve. The Talented Tenth, as he called it, had never experienced so glowing or majestic a social event as this wedding. But even someone as wise and experienced as Du Bois could be wrong in some of the particulars. While the wedding was a spectacular achievement, the marriage was far less satisfying.

Fall from Grace

While thousands of people were thrilled to witness the joining of Harlem's brightest literary star and the daughter of its most formidable thinker and political leader, the relationship had critical problems.

Separate Paths

Right from the beginning, there were strains in the marital relationship. The couple honeymooned briefly in Atlantic City, but Yolande Cullen had to return to Baltimore, to complete her high school teaching year. To most observers, it made sense that Cullen accompany his bride to Baltimore, but he was soon back in Harlem, taking up residence with his adoptive parents.

In July, just three months after the wedding, Countee Cullen embarked for France on what was presumably an extension of their earlier shortened honeymoon. He went with his adoptive father—and his dear friend Harold Jackman. On the outside, Cullen had a good reason. He

Yolande Du Bois and Countee Cullen had a short honeymoon in Atlantic City, before Cullen all but abandoned his new wife.

had won a fellowship from the renowned Guggenheim Foundation, and he had already planned to spend the fellowship year in France. But the embarkation without his new bride caused no end of stir in the black community. Yolande would join them a couple of months later, but the emotional and physical disconnect between the newlyweds was readily apparent.

If the difficulties had been restricted to the marriage bed, the young couple might have made it. But there were temperamental, as well as social and sexual differences. Yolande was jealous of her husband's affection. For his part, Countee was jealous of her time. They seemed to have ignored these difficulties during the courtship.

Have some couples made it through a rocky beginning to emerge as powerfully united? To be sure. The people whom Countee and Yolande asked for advice were almost unanimous in declaring that early married life requires adjustment, and that the couple should stick it out. But, for many reasons, including Cullen's unaddressed sexuality, this particular couple did not possess a strong foundation. What had previously been whispers and rumors now became shouts, as many African Americans—of high station and low—declared this was a poor beginning to married life.

A Failed Effort

Countee Cullen sought more advice from his father-in-law than his adoptive father. W. E. B. Du Bois was very fond of Countee, and he wanted the marriage to work. Du Bois's letters indicate that he sympathized more with his son-in-law than his daughter. Even his efforts failed, however.

Less than two years after the wedding, Countee Cullen and Yolande Du Bois were divorced. Divorce was neither common nor readily available in the America of 1928, so the legal proceedings took place in Paris. Countee pleaded no contest to the charge of spousal abandonment. That they shared no significant property, or children, made matters easier. By the summer of 1930, Cullen was a free man once more.

He was also free to contemplate the ruin of his social life.

Consolation in Paris

Cullen sought refuge from all his marital problems in Paris. In the summer of 1928, while his marriage was just beginning, he sailed from New York, and he spent much of the following three years in the French capital. Many things had proved disappointing, but it was not the case with Paris. Cullen was simply thrilled with the place and its people.

Cullen came to Paris at precisely the right time—as the Harlem Renaissance was winding down. The stock market crash had not yet happened, but there was already an exodus of talent from New York to Paris.

Cullen made many friends in Paris. Among them was Augusta Savage, the renowned African American sculptress. Like Cullen, she had experienced a painful upbringing; unlike him, Savage continued to battle financial difficulty throughout life. The two hit it off right away. The same can be said of Cullen and Stephen and Sophie Victor Greene. This wealthy American couple smoothed Cullen's path, allowing him to attend many high-priced parties: they

After the breakup of his marriage, Cullen found solace in the beauty of Paris.

also brought him to the French Riviera. As a result, Cullen looked back on his two years in Paris as among the best times of his life. Years later, he paid tribute to the city, and nation, in "To France":

> I have a dream of where (when I grow old,
>> Having no further joy to take in lip
> Or limb, a graybeard catching from the cold
>> The frail indignity of age) some ship
> Might bear my creaking, unhinged bones
>> Trailing remembrance as a tattered cloak,
> And beach me glad, though on their sharpest stones
>> Among a fair and kindly foreign folk.[1]

Paris, and France, remained one of the great, lasting loves of Cullen's life.

Picking Up the Pieces

Countee Cullen came home to Harlem in 1931. The years he had spent in France were delightful. But the homecoming was a hard one. Cullen returned just as the Great Depression entered its cruelest phase.

African Americans in the Great Depression

The Depression imposed such hardships that few people—of that time or our own—wish to compare among the various miseries. That said, it seems inarguable that black citizens, oppressed even in the best of times, would be suffering more dramatically than most.

Three generations had passed since the Emancipation Proclamation, but systemic discrimination of the African American community meant that black men and women still had to struggle hard to enter the working and middle-class of American society. Many black citizens were approaching middle-class economic positions when the Great Depression struck, in 1929, and they were

The Great Depression hit Harlem and its residents hard.

among the first to be laid off. Though African Americans were more accustomed to hardship, that did not make the economic misery of the 1930s any easier to bear.

Countee Cullen was spared much of this distress. As the son of Reverend Frederick Cullen, he would always have a place to sleep, at the very least. But the Great Depression did curtail Cullen's job prospects.

An Unexpected Role

Of all the people who knew Cullen at the height of his career, virtually none would have selected, or predicted, the role of public school teacher. In the 1920s, Cullen seemed destined either to be a university professor, or an independent writer, and that he would live well in either case. But the Great Depression plus the loss of patrons (some never forgave him for the divorce from Yolande Du Bois) meant Cullen could not pick and choose. In 1932, he became a substitute teacher in the New York City school system, and in 1934 he won a

Even the apartment building where both Cullen and W. E. B. Du Bois lived fell victim to the Depression, as the owners, the once wealthy Rockefellers, failed to keep up with the property's payments.

full-time appointment, as teacher of English and French, at Frederick Douglass Junior High.

Many literary lions, such as Walt Whitman and Herman Melville, have been forced to toil in occupations to support their writing. In Cullen's case, however, the very activities of his job—the many hours devoted to students and their assignments—made it nearly impossible for him to write. For a time, Cullen accepted the situation, and made the best of it. One student later recalled the effectiveness of Cullen's instruction:

> Because he...had a method of teaching which [was] probably unusual. He taught us...there's nothing you can't read and there's nothing you can't do...And what he would do, take out the class and we'd walk around a block, a city block and come back. He'd say "I want you to write down everything you saw"...And we did that every day for a month and at the end of a month we were supposed to be able to draw every building and write down every street number.[1]

For a teacher of English and French, this was a highly unusual routine, but one can see its effectiveness. Cullen taught his young charges to trust their own eyes and ears, to accustom their minds to seeing and understanding.

The Medea

Cullen worked hard, both in teaching and his poetry. In 1935, Harper & Brothers brought out his fourth major work, *The Medea and Some Poems*. Cullen's translation of *The Medea* from the Greek, was solid, and won some applause. But as a poet, he was naturally graded, or assessed, on the quality of his poems, and those found in *The Medea* were not well regarded by critics.

Was there an exception to the general rule? If so, it was found in "Any Human to Another, " wherein he dwelled upon the significance of human connection through sorrow, writing that "Your grief and mine/ Must intertwine/ Like

Actress Dorothy Ateca performs in a 1940 production based on Countee Cullen's translation of *The Medea*.

sea and river,/ Be fused and mingle,/ Diverse yet single,/ Forever and forever."[2]

Even as he adjusted to a new line of work and continued to work as a poet, Cullen also made a bid for personal happiness.

An End to His Beginning

Cullen had long kept the story of his birth mother and father private. Very likely, he did not know very much about them. But sometime in the 1930s, he began sending a monthly check to his birth mother, who lived in Louisville, Kentucky (it seems he did not tell his adoptive father). When his mother died, in 1940, Cullen made a special trip to Louisville to arrange for her burial and the disposal of her effects. This appears to have freed him to make another major move, this time in the direction of marriage.

A Second Marriage

Ida Mae Roberson was about as different from Yolande Du Bois as can be imagined. While Du Bois came from prominence and a bit of wealth, Roberson came from humble circumstances. Countee Cullen met Roberson in the 1930s, as she was headed toward a divorce. Their friendship turned to admiration, and Cullen began a slow, deliberate courtship. By 1940, when Cullen made a formal proposal, the pair had known each other for ten years. Cullen proposed by letter, and the document survives, giving us a good idea of his understanding, and how he had advanced since his first, failed, marriage.

> If you are willing to overlook and understand my deficiencies, and are not to be too disgusted by a husband who can't stand the lightning, there isn't any reason why we shouldn't be happy…You must think it over very carefully and be sure that you won't have any cause for regret.[3]

Roberson accepted (her return letter has not survived). The couple was married at Salem Methodist Church, with Cullen's adoptive father presiding. It was a very small affair, however, altogether different from Cullen's wedding to Yolande De Bois.

How much Cullen told his new wife of his sexuality remains unknown, though one wonders if his warning about his deficiencies and his admonition to "think it over carefully," was a gentle indicator. One thing is certain, however—Cullen's second marriage was much happier than his first. And his allusion to "the lightning" in the proposal letter was later born out. On a trip to Fisk University, in 1944, Cullen was so terrified by a series of lightning strikes that he had to hide in his hotel room.

Physical Infirmities

Cullen was not in good, or even decent, health. He turned forty in 1943, when the Second World War was in full swing, and was already plagued by a number of ailments. He suffered frequent headaches, and his blood pressure was alarmingly high (there were, as yet, no good drugs to mediate high blood pressure).

One is tempted to imagine that Cullen's physical distress was a symptom of his depression, and that the depression was itself caused by his lack of success with the pen. No

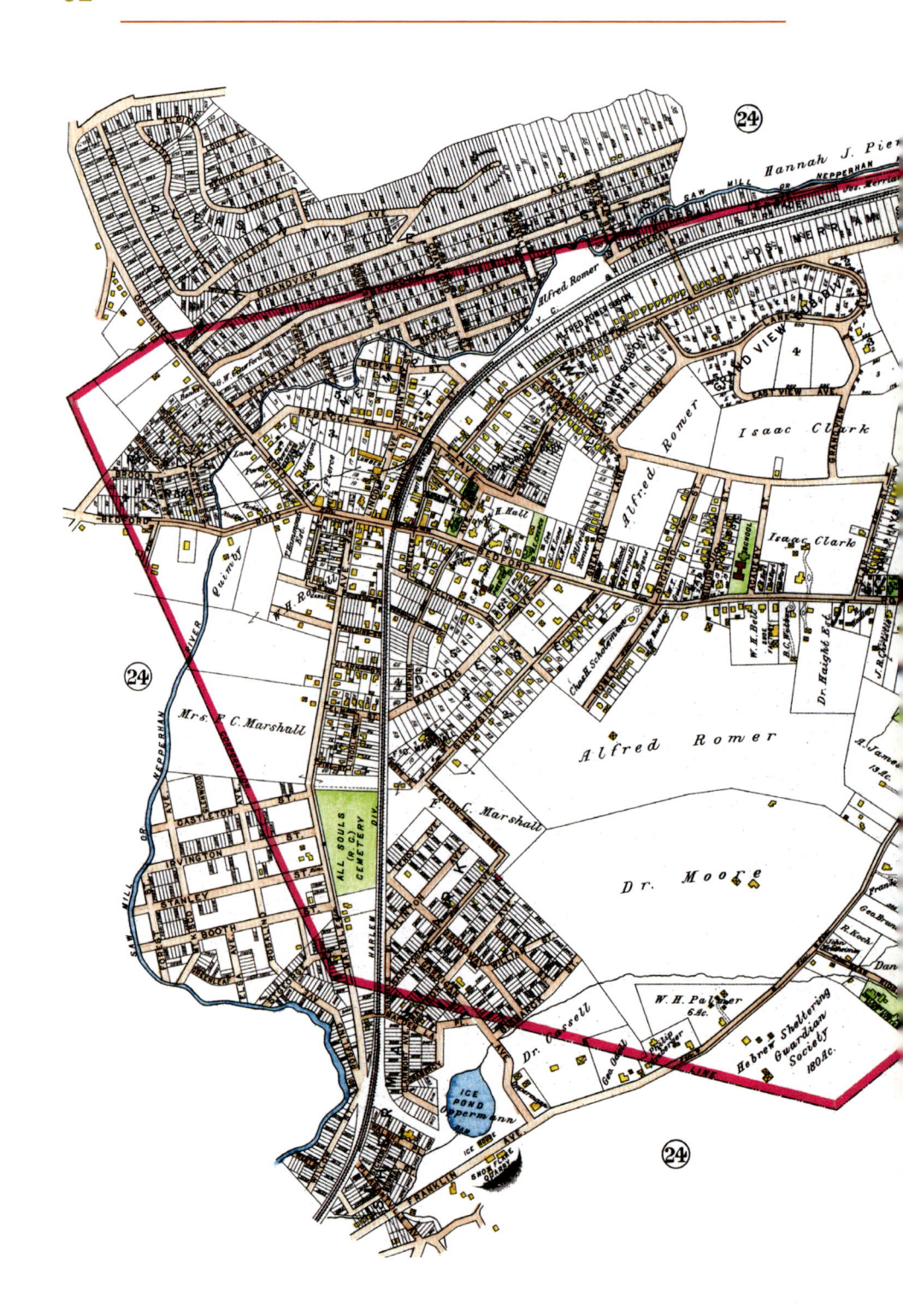

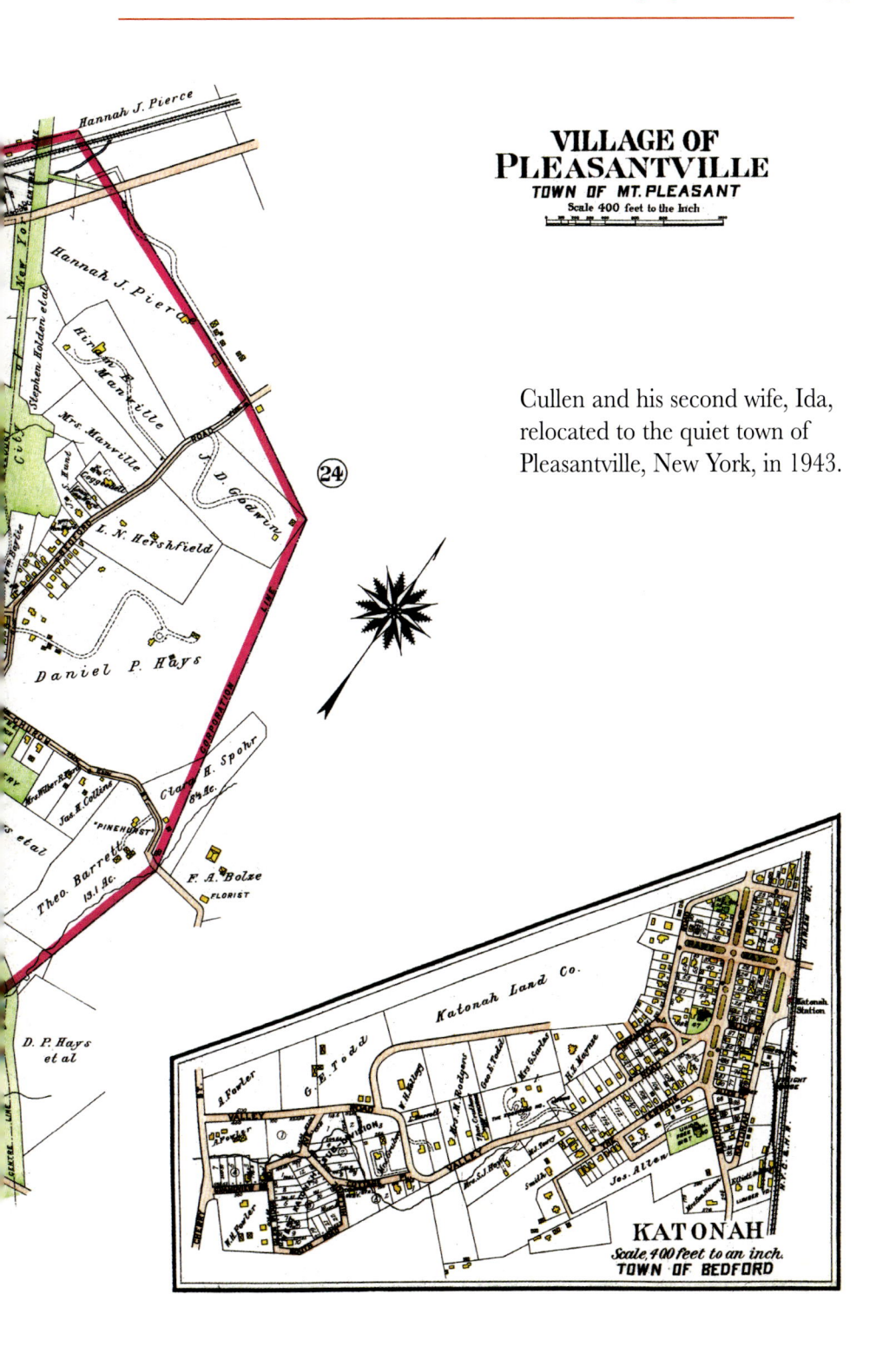

VILLAGE OF
PLEASANTVILLE
TOWN OF MT. PLEASANT
Scale 400 feet to the inch

Cullen and his second wife, Ida, relocated to the quiet town of Pleasantville, New York, in 1943.

KATONAH
Scale 400 feet to an inch.
TOWN OF BEDFORD

significant publication came after his translation of *Medea* in 1935. Then, too, his many hours at Frederick Douglass Junior High took a significant toll.

Hoping to address both issues, Cullen and his wife decided to move to the suburbs. They found a modest home in Pleasantville, New York, moving there in 1943. For a few short months, Cullen was more relaxed than at any previous time. He liked living with plenty of trees nearby, and taking the subway into New York City was a surprising delight. But a short time after moving to Pleasantville, Cullen and his wife had to take in his reverend father, whose health was failing.

Frederick Cullen had been a widower since 1932. He managed to continue preaching and running Salem Methodist for nearly a decade, but then collapsed from the strain. He came to live with his son and daughter-in-law, and she seems to have been of tremendous comfort to him. For Countee, however, his father's arrival spelled an increase in the family expenses, and served as a warning about what their future might be.

Facing financial difficulty, Cullen dusted off a work he had written years earlier. *St. Louis Woman* was a musical, written in collaboration with Arna Bontemps. Working feverishly, the co-authors managed to attract attention from producers willing to finance the show, and in July 1945, Countee made an important trip west to meet with them. To be a "has-been" poet was difficult, even painful. But if Cullen could rebuild his career as a writer for the theatre, all might be well.

10

Legacy

Countee Cullen spent several months in California, and he became enamored of the Golden State's scenery. Virtually his entire life had been spent on the East Coast, and like many another traveler, writer, or combination of the two, Cullen liked what he found in California. But if the scenery was delightful, the strains of getting the musical off the ground were not.

Cullen had always seen himself as a serious writer, and *St. Louis Woman* was a foray into a lighter genre. He had written the first draft seven or eight years earlier, however, and his writing did not wear well in 1945: it had all the marks of a 1930s or even 1920s musical. For once in his career, Cullen experimented and played, and the results were not what he hoped for.

Lena Horne, the most successful African American actress of the decade, turned down the leading role since the heroine was a woman of "easy virtue." Other actors and actresses followed suit. Cullen and Arna Bontemps worked frantically to make the script and scenes

With the book written by Cullen and Arna Bontemps and the music written by Harold Arlen and Johnny Mercer, *St. Louis Woman* opened in March of 1946, just a few months after Cullen's death.

more current, appropriate to a Second World War audience. Cullen was troubled by news from home, however. His wife sent him frequent letters and telegrams, updating him on his father's poor health. On top of everything else, Cullen and his wife were preparing to sell their house in Pleasantville.

Given the distractions, and conflicts, it is not surprising Countee Cullen's health began to deteriorate. He had not been well for years, but 1945 represented the worst time thus far. Returning home in the autumn of 1945, Cullen attempted to put things together. But he was weak, and increasingly disoriented. In January 1946, he was hospitalized in New York City, where he died on January 21.

Those Left Behind

At the time of Cullen's death, he was deeply concerned with the fate of two people—his father and his second wife. Reverend Frederick Cullen survived Countee Cullen only by a few months, and with his death, the small, tight-knit family was gone.

Ida Roberson Cullen lived several more decades. Though she married again, and took her new husband's name, her devotion to Countee Cullen only became more pronounced. She organized numerous readings in her late husband's honor and did all she could to keep his name in front of the newspapers and magazines. Her sterling efforts took a long time to bear fruit.

Of all the poets and writers of prose Cullen knew in his lifetime, only one could be counted on to deliver a fair assessment. W. E. B. Du Bois said some stirring words about Cullen, and Alain Locke delivered a fair assessment at the funeral. But only Langston Hughes really came through for his old friend. "Creative writers sometimes have long periods of silence," Hughes asserted. "Had he lived he might have written beautifully and brilliantly again."[1]

Hughes was generous to his long-time friend and sometime rival. Many other critics were more negative in their assessment. Cullen's long silence (*The Medea* was published ten years prior to his death) suggested to them that his best days for writing had come and gone.

A Last Appraisal

How does Countee Cullen stack up among the poets of his time? How does he rate among the African American poets of the twentieth century?

In sheer talent, he was second to none. When *Color* was published in 1925, Cullen appeared to be the African American poet of his generation, and a contender for that place among white writers as well. But the potential

COUNTEE CULLEN
1903 - 1946

AND WHEN YOUR BODY'S DEATH GIVES BIRTH
TO SOIL FOR SPRING TO CROWN,
MEN WILL NOT ASK IF THAT RARE EARTH
WAS WHITE FLESH ONCE, OR BROWN.

Though he lived for only a brief time, Countee Cullen's contributions to poetry are great and enduring.

shown in *Color* was never equaled. *Copper Sun* is a fine book of poems and *Medea* is a first-rate translation. Neither was different enough from other books on the market to make a sensation. One hates to say it, but Cullen had created lightning in a bottle with *Color*—a phenomenon that was nearly impossible to recreate in later years.

Did it have to be this way? Could Cullen have recovered? Perhaps without the grand spectacle of his first marriage and divorce, it might have been possible. His failed relationship with Yolande Du Bois put him on a downward track from which he never recovered. The Guggenheim fellowship year in Paris was filled with personal success, but he was unable to recapture the spark of his early years. Though this was a difficult unfolding of circumstances, perhaps the healthiest perspective on such a turn of fortune comes from Cullen himself: "There is no secret to success except hard work and getting something indefinable which we call 'the breaks.'"[2]

Though Countee Cullen may have been handed a few tough breaks—a less-than-ideal early childhood, a sexuality he'd need to conceal, a very high-profile divorce—he nonetheless left this world as a towering figure in the Harlem Renaissance and in American poetry.

Chronology

1903
Cullen is born in Louisville, Kentucky.

1910
Cullen is in New York City, living with his grandmother, Amanda Porter.

1917
Amanda Porter dies.
The United States enters the First World War.

1918
Cullen is informally adopted by Reverend and Mrs. Frederick A. Cullen.
"To the Swimmer" is printed in a high school magazine.

1920
"I Have a Rendezvous with Life" is published and often reprinted.

1922
Cullen enters NYU.

1925
Color is published by Harper & Brothers.

1926
Cullen earns his master's degree from Harvard.

1926
Cullen and his adoptive father make their first trip to Europe.
Copper Sun, Cullen's second book of poems, is published.

1928
Cullen marries Yolande Du Bois.

He leaves for France, on a Guggenheim fellowship.

1930

Cullen and Yolande Du Bois divorce.

1931

Yolande Du Bois remarries.

1933

Cullen begins teaching in New York City public schools.

1935

The Medea and Some Poems is published.

1940

Cullen arranges for his birth mother's funeral.

1940

Cullen marries Ida Marie Roberson.

1945

Cullen travels to California to arrange for stage production of *St. Louis Woman.*

1946

Cullen dies in January.
Reverend Frederick Cullen dies in May.

Chapter Notes

Chapter 1
Pained Youth

1. Major Jackson, Ed., *Countee Cullen: Collected Poems* (New York: Library of America, 2013), pp. 15–16.
2. Countee Cullen, *Color* (Harper & Brothers, 1925), p. 46.

Chapter 2
A New Life

1. Reverend Frederick Asbury Cullen, *From Barefoot Town to Jerusalem* (Private printing, 1946), p. 13.
2. Cullen, p. 29.
3. Cullen, p. 39.
4. Cullen, p. 10.
5. Cullen, p. 11.

Chapter 3
Prodigy

1. Major Jackson, *Countee Cullen: Collected Poems* (New York: Library of America, 2013), p. 235.
2. Jackson, p. 236.

Chapter 4
Recognition

1. Michael Lucius Lomax, "Countee Cullen: From the Dark Tower," unpublished PhD dissertation, 1984, p. 69.
2. Countee Cullen, *Color* (New York: Harper & Brothers, 1925), p. 10.

Chapter 5
Color

1. Countee Cullen, *Color* (New York: Harper & Brothers, 1925), p. 15.
2. Cullen, pp. 24–25.
3. Cullen, p. 26.
4. Cullen, p. 30
5. Gerald Early, Ed., *My Soul's High Song: The Collected Writings of Countee Cullen* (New York: Doubleday, 1991), p. 38.

Chapter 6
The Summit

1. Reverend Frederick Asbury Cullen, *From Barefoot Town to Jerusalem* (Private printing, 1946), p. 15.
2. Ibid.
3. Charles Molesworth. *And Bid Him Sing: A Biography of Countee Cullen* (Chicago: The University of Chicago Press, 2012), p. 102.
4. Countee Cullen. *Copper Sun* (New York: Harper & Brothers, 1927), p. 3.
5. W. E. B. Du Bois, "So the Girl Marries," *The Crisis,* June 1928, pp. 192–193, 208.

Chapter 7
Wedding of the Decade

1. Thelma E. Berlack, "Miss Du Bois Weds: Wedding Guests Sans Invitations Arrive Very Early," *New York Amsterdam News,* April 11, 1928, p. 6.
2. Ibid.
3. W. E. B. Du Bois, "So the Girl Marries," *The Crisis,* June 1928, pp. 208–209.

Chapter 8
Fall from Grace

1. Countee Cullen, *The Medea* (New York: Harper & Brothers, 1935), p. 74.

Chapter 9
Picking Up the Pieces

1. Charles Molesworth, *And Bid Him Sing: A Biography of Countee Cullen* (Chicago: University of Chicago Press, 2012,) p. 204.
2. "Any Human to Another," *The Medea and Some Poems* (New York: Harper & Brothers, 1935), pp. 70–71.
3. Michael Lucius Lomax, "Countee Cullen: From the Dark Tower," unpublished Ph.D dissertation, 1984, p. 266.

Chapter 10
Legacy

1. Michael Lucius Lomax, "Countee Cullen: From the Dark Tower," unpublished PhD dissertation, 1984, pp. 292–293.
2. Lionel C. Bascom, Ed., *Voices of the African American Experience* (Westport, CT: Greenwood Press, 2009), p. 504.

Glossary

codified Formally approved and enforced by law.

formidable Strong; powerful.

gender performance Manner or style of dress one selects to act out masculinity or femininity.

Harlem Renaissance Artistic, political, and cultural movement from roughly 1920–1930 that saw the rapid rise of black artists in all disciplines, centered mostly around the neighborhood of Harlem in New York City.

indefatigable Never tiring or wearing out.

institutional racism Racism that is often enforced by social, political, and governmental structures, such as the oppression of African Americans by segregation, and housing and job discrimination.

obscurity A state of being unknown to the general public.

parsonage A house given to a member of the clergy, usually a minister.

prodigious Possessing great size or importance.

prolific Highly productive.

Rhodes Scholar An award given to outstanding postgraduates, allowing them to study at the prestigious University of Oxford.

segregation A practice that separated men and women based on their race that formally ended with the Civil Rights Act of 1964.

Talented Tenth A belief held by W. E. B. Du Bois that the black community in America would be uplifted by a Talented Tenth of select black men and women who were well educated and committed to fighting for political change.

tertiary Third in order or importance.

Further Reading

BOOKS

Jackson, Major., Ed. *Countee Cullen: Collected Poems*. New York, NY: Library of America, 2013.

Molesworth, Charles. *And Bid Him Sing: A Biography of Countee Cullen*. Chicago, IL: University of Chicago Press, 2012.

Orr, Tamra B. *The Harlem Renaissance: An African American Cultural Movement*. New York, NY: Lucent Press, 2018.

WEBSITES

Countee Cullen | Poems
https://www.poemhunter.com/countee-cullen/
A collection of Countee Cullen's poems.

Countee Cullen | Poetry Foundation
https://www.poetryfoundation.org/poets/countee-cullen
An in-depth profile of Countee Cullen.

Countee Cullen Reads
https://www.youtube.com/watch?v=UvN96fn5xTE
A recording of Countee Cullen reading his poem "Heritage."

Index

Charlotte
Etinde-Crompton

Samuel
Willard Crompton

About the Authors

Charlotte Etinde-Crompton was born and raised in Zaire and came to Massachusetts at the age of twenty. Her artistic sensibility stems from her early exposure to the many talented artists of her family and tribe, which included master wood-carvers. Her interest in African American art has been an abiding passion since her arrival in the United States.

Samuel Willard Crompton is a tenth-generation New Englander who now lives in metropolitan Atlanta. For twenty-eight years, he was professor of history at Holyoke Community College. His early interest in the arts comes from his wood-carver father and his oil-painter mother. Crompton is the author and editor of many books, including a number of nonfiction young adult titles with Enslow Publishing. This is his first collaboration with his wife.